MY STORY TIME.

AUNT ALICE

TELMA GUIMARÃES

Illustrated by Alejandro Rosas

Editora Saraiva

AUNT

THIS IS AUNT ALICE.

BED

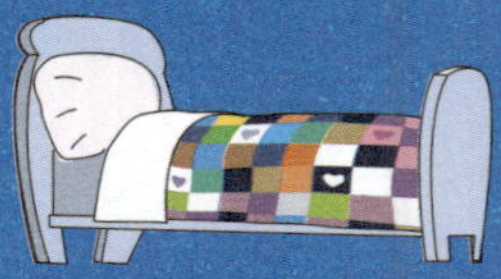

SHE'S IN BED NOW.

CAT

THIS IS HER CAT, YOLANDA.

DOG

AND THIS IS HER DOG, WILLY.

EVENING

IT'S EVENING AND THE PETS WANT TO EAT.

FOOD

"WHAT KIND OF FOOD?"
SHE ASKS.

GOOD FOOD!

"SOMETHING GOOD!" THEY THINK.

HUNGRY

"WE'RE HUNGRY!"
THE DOG BARKS AND
THE CAT MEOWS.

ICE-CREAM

"I WANT SOME ICE-CREAM!" YOLANDA MEOWS.

JELLY

"I PREFER SOME JELLY!"
BARKS WILLY.

KITCHEN

"LET'S GO TO THE KITCHEN!" AUNT ALICE DECIDES.

LADY-BUG

"LEAVE THE LADY-BUG ALONE!" AUNT ALICE ASKS THE PETS.

MEATBALLS

"THIS IS YOUR MEAL:
MEATBALLS..."
SHE SHOWS WILLY.

NOSE

"DON'T PUT YOUR NOSE
IN THE FOOD!"
SHE TELLS THE PUPPY.

OSTRICH

YOU LOOK LIKE AN OSTRICH!

PAIL

"A PAIL FULL OF MILK?"
THE KITTY SHOWS THE PAIL.

QUEEN

"YOU LOOK LIKE A QUEEN!"
AUNT ALICE LAUGHS
AT YOLANDA.

RIBBON

"COME HERE!
LET ME TIE YOU A RIBBON!"
AUNT ALICE CALLS THE KITTY.

SNOWMAN

"LET'S GO OUTSIDE
TO SEE THE SNOWMAN!"
SHE CALLS THE PETS.

TURTLE

"OK, COME ON MRS. TURTLE!"

UMBRELLA

"NO, SHE DOESN'T NEED AN UMBRELLA!"

VELVET

"HERE'S YOUR VELVET COAT, WILLY!"

XMAS

IT'S CHRISTMAS TIME FOR...

YOLANDA, WILLY AND ZIGZAG.

THE AUTHOR

My name is **Telma Guimarães**. I was born in Marília, São Paulo. When I was a teenager, I took an Exchange program in Covington, Georgia. It was a wonderful experience. I graduated with a bachelor degree in Languages, English and Literature at UNESP. I moved to Campinas and then I started teaching English. I have three children and I loved telling stories to my kids. Many of the stories were created by me.
My heart was always full of joy when I sat on my chair and thought about children, animals, nature and so on. So, I gave up teaching and tried to reach my goal: to be an author. Here I am.

A1
A2
B1
B2
C1
C2

Quadro Europeu Comum de Referência para Línguas (CEFR)

AUNT ALICE

Presidência
Mario Ghio Júnior

Vice-presidência de educação digital
Camila Montero Vaz Cardoso

Direção editorial
Lidiane Vivaldini Olo

Gerência editorial
Julio Cesar Augustus de Paula Santos

Coordenação editorial
Laura Vecchioli do Prado

Aprendizagem digital
Renata Galdino (ger.), Beatriz de Almeida Pinto Rodrigues da Costa (coord. Experiência de Aprendizagem), Carla Isabel Ferreira Reis (coord. Produção Multimídia), Daniella dos Santos Di Nubila (coord. Produção Digital), Rogerio Fabio Alves (coord. Publicação), Vanessa Tavares Menezes de Souza (coord. Design Digital)

Planejamento, controle de produção e indicadores
Flávio Matuguma (ger.), Juliana Batista (coord.) e Jayne Ruas (analista

Edição
Instituto Parole

Revisão
Ray Shoulder e Maria Claudia Franchi

Ilustração, projeto gráfico e diagramação
Alejandro Rosas

Capa
Thatiana Kalaes

Editora Saraiva

CL: 531266
CAE: 795104

2022
1ª edição
1ª tiragem
Impressão e acabamento: Bartira

Direitos desta edição cedidos à Somos Sistemas de Ensino S.A.
Av. Paulista, 901, Bela Vista
São Paulo – SP – CEP 01310-200
Tel.: (0xx11) 4003-3061

Conheça o nosso portal de literatura Coletivo Leitor:
www.coletivoleitor.com.br

Dados Internacionais de Catalogação na Publicação (CIP)

Guimarães, Telma
Aunt Alice / Telma Guimarães
Ilustrações de Alejandro Rosas.
1. ed. – São Paulo : Saraiva, 2022.

ISBN 978-65-5867-109-1

1. Literatura infantojuvenil I. Título II. Rosas, Alejandro

22-2927

Angélica Ilacqua - Bibliotecária - CRB-8/7057

Este livro foi composto nas fontes Arial, Raleway e fontes do próprio ilustrador e impresso sobre papel off set 90 g/m2.